GOING HOME

GOING HOME

A poetry collection

Rick Andreoli

To order additional copies of this book, contact:
Xlibris Corporation
1-888-795-4274
www.Xlibris.com
Orders@Xlibris.com
21098

CONTENTS

In Loving Memory, to Fred "Mister" Rogers,
the kind man from Pittsburgh,
who changed the world with his smile.

"GOING HOME"

The wooded lot intrigued me still,
With its gleaming reveries of shade,
A brief hiatus from toil and till,
In sandy paths of mysterious cascades.

Toward the end of an infinite haze,
Mossy grass gave repose for my soul,
Cicadas and crickets sang their praise,
The golden robin stood proudly extolled.

Under the canopy I began to feel free,
Tranquility was nature's preferred pace,
Young saplings branched out of hardy seeds,
Dark corridors of old secrets were traced.

A carriage house stood unpretentiously,
Nothing stirred as I listened for a sound,
A fiery sun glowed behind prickly leaves,
Shades of gray snuck in all around.

Fluttering memories came up with a rush,
The moldy garage appeared rearranged,
Darkness came now and the trees were hushed,
As I walked toward the old window pane.

I dreamily climbed the collapsing old steps,
The leafy porch missed part of its railing,
The living room appeared sparsely kept,
A ceiling fan went ominously sailing.

I briefly knocked for the bell was detached,
A weak screen door could use some repair,
I inquired in but my voice wasn't matched,
An open door tempted me to enter there.

Crossing the threshold into shadows unknown,
A circular mirror beckoned me from the right,
The reflection I saw had a singular tone,
To the kitchen I quickly alighted.

A side entrance revealed no car on the drive,
Blinding spotlights brought on mothy throngs,
Not one person was there to confide,
And the clock on the wall was far gone.

I turned toward the gloomy and gothic stairway,
Something told me I must go upstairs,
Bravely ascending to where dreams were made,
A hallway lamp now eerily glared.

Each room I observed no sign to be found,
Deja'vu came as I slowly crept,
Fear gave way when I heard a strange sound,
I returned through the creaky, old cleft.

One last door now affected my mind,
I softly opened it though trembling inside,
The stairs angled high as I surveyed behind,
The narrow attic was waiting to abide.

Ancient, deep thoughts now entered my heart,
The inward journey must somehow conclude,
Arriving on top, I suddenly made a start,
Anxious moments began to exude.

Slanted dark walls and a childhood long past,
By the window I once again stood,
But years had passed and days went fast,
It was hard now to see what was good.

Suddenly a truck came with beaming lights,
I flew down the tall flights of stairs,
Landing on the porch in the sultry night,
Getting out was my last major care.

Cars flew by on the dusty, black road,
Massive maples swallowed up the old shack,
Finally I had faced my burdening load,
And I knew that I'd never go back.

"SANDPIPER, SANDPIPER"

Sandpiper, sandpiper,
My petite and vibrant friend,
How gracefully you glide by the surf late at night,
Your energetic movements are an august delight.

You and the rest of your dancing night flock,
Perform a cheerful ballet at the end of the day,
Like champion skaters vaulting into the air,
I silently approach to see how you fare.

You refuse to stand idle for a very long time,
Many attempts I have made to get near you,
Your sprinter's feet, faster than the eye sees,
Your lovely night waltz is a flicker of glee.

The promenade continues on the quiet sandy beach,
As a curtain moon arises over the deep and dark stage,
The acrobatic performers silently beseech me,
Does life have a meaning tell us now very quickly.

Who am I to answer such questions,
So profound and very deep,
Let's face the gale bravely,
While releasing our cares,
The future will have its moments,
The eternity we now share.

"MY SEARCH"

Not one singular man truly knows,
The infinite essence of life,
Uncanny feelings give hints to the soul,
But the real blueprints are unknown to us all.

The cycle of a droplet is a marvelous thing,
As it saunters its way down a pedal,
I have little doubt of its rippling to the ground,
And finding its destiny en route heaven-bound.

My inner joy is a great blessing I know,
In a boisterous mad-driven world,
Silent prophetic words on the page,
Enlighten my thoughts to an elevated stage.

The mysterious journey for knowledge is endless,
Though time hastens forward expiring,
The blossoming temple within my kind mind,
Has a tempest of heartfelt emotion entwined.

I'm certain that life in itself equals love,
I cherish all God's great creations,
Long live all of my joyful own,
The seeds of spring shall again be sown.

"MOMENTS"

I'm savoring precious moments in time,
Watching the wind reflect the sunshine,
Through ruffled, delicate needles of pine,
The cold winter air is a little unkind.

Cascading streams bring beauty to all,
Mossy shade trees grow dark green and tall,
Mountains form valleys and patches of land,
Cozy quaint farmhouses poignantly stand.

Each changing nuance of life intrigues me,
The ongoing flow of a sandy beached sea,
Tiny sandpipers run fast from the waves,
Glistening bays foray into dark caves.

Each of these moments can entwine my soul,
Showing me ways to make sense of it all,
A gentle spring night shortly after a rain,
The warm moistened air makes me well once again.

Every sunrise is a fresh dewy gift,
The seasons pass by and the ivy will shift,
These heartfelt and colorful memories persist,
The moments I had and the moments I missed.

"BETTER DAYS"

Oh the tears you'll cry my child,
But soon they'll dry and days turn mild,
A thousand worries will fade into blue,
A gentle spring-like breeze for you.

Your heart will forge a newfound way,
A dedication here to stay,
Where kind and gentle thoughts bestow,
The greatest days you'll ever know.

The child within will run and sing,
Exploring each mysterious thing,
The blossoming road turns green again,
The sun becomes your dearest friend.

The robin sings his heartfelt song,
On soft and thawing April lawns,
Today is like no other one,
A whole new you has just begun.

"SATURDAY"

I sometimes hear the whistle,
Of the rumbling, midnight train,
It brings me back into the past,
With its vast, expansive echo,
The monumental shaking,
Of the journeying railway cars,
Brings me to a dreamy state,
That reaches to my heart.

Those lazy special times,
On an April Saturday morning,
Reading the back of a cereal box,
While staring into the yard,
Watching early shows,
In the little plywood shack,
An orange glowing sun,
Was bringing springtime back.

Slanted, dusty rays,
Now warmed the chilly room,
I never missed Gene London's,
Cartoon Corner General Store,
Old Mr. Quigley paid him,
Just three cents a week,
A tunnel led to the mansion,
Where goblins liked to creep.

The robin's song was boisterous,
On those cozy, April days,
Reading Mad magazines,
Or the cover of Abbey Road,
Our brown weedy lawn,
Was where my friends would play,
We'd climb the gray magnolia,
And hide in the shade.

Later in the day,
We'd bike to Fairmount Park,
The Japanese garden,
Was mysteriously alluring,
We'd ride the shallow canals,
Near the trolley in Havertown,
Then we'd coast the bus-line,
Heading homeward bound.

Those lovely Saturdays,
Were filled with sunny joy,
All the lawny vistas,
And winding, hilly roads,
Sometimes Gramps would take us,
To the house of Audubon,
We'd hike through shady valleys,
And in meadows we would run.

Back at home our Mother's,
Deep emotions would succumb,
She had to go away,
This was all that could be done,
Nana came to stay,
As our lives became surreal,
She packed my Monkees lunchbox,
With amazing skill.

We'd cross the tracks on Saturday,
To see a horror show,
Playing on the elevators,
At the Suburban Square Mall,
The adventures still continued,
Even though she wasn't there,
Sometimes we'd go visit her,
In the middle of nowhere.

May brought lush greenery,
With overreaching trees,
The rosebuds by the porch,
Had embraced the summer sun,
We heard that this Saturday,
Mom was coming home,
Babylonian chariots,
And forts of Ancient Rome.

We continued playing in,
The narrow alleyways,
Car wheels kicked up stone,
When the car pulled in with Mom,
She looked so beautiful,
With her wavy auburn hair,
Home at last we thought,
With compassion everywhere.

"HOME"

A homey life I like the most,
A picket fence and cinnamon toast,
Winding walks on meadowed streets,
Where stingray bikes and lovers meet.

A fireplace on a snowy night,
With yuletide warmth and sparkly lights,
A pumpkin pie and gingerbread man,
Smiling faces close at hand.

The back-yard corner old oak tree,
On Saturdays we meet with glee,
The ringing bells of old shop doors,
A starry glistening night-time tour.

Exuberant joy of a first snowfall,
The howling wind's deep wondrous call,
Sculpted drifty angel flakes,
A Mallard on a frozen lake.

A crescent man-on-moon ascends,
As crunchy tires turn the bend,
A horse-sleigh greets a sunset sky,
The lamp-lit town sits closely by.

"THE GIFT"

Life should be a leafy bliss,
Each blue sky a red silk stocking,
Every breath of summer air,
A bird-winged eternity knocking.

The hilly tree-lined scenery,
Enlivens my heart each day,
Every wink a wondrous gift,
Where childhood dreams can stay.

Resplendent light from an orange sun,
Reflects to the red brick street,
A piney olive mountain view,
With a railway line at its feet.

A shady Indian summer breeze,
In a riverbank genre painting,
A sunny and lawny solitude,
Where optimism always is reigning.

Today it feels as if all things,
Have a meaningful purpose and place,
A shrubby hill with a steep, stone path,
Where a tulip tree can be traced.

The home fire burns within my breast,
The apple cider warms my soul,
All things are good when understood,
Then life can never be old.

"UP ABOVE"

The advent of my soul was swift,
When I looked to the breaking heavens,
The miraculous sight of paradise,
Brought with it bright blue skies.

These empyreal sights amazed me,
As I watched phosphorescent beams,
Large and fluffy floating clouds,
Became redemptive snowy shrouds.

For what's more forgiving than a clearing sky,
With a twilight moon looming up so high,
As a glowing sun turns the ground to steam,
And the rippling puddles a reflective sheen.

As night approaches the sky is streaked,
With etched-on clouds and a lavender goodbye,
The mysteries of life continue to grow,
The longer I live the less that I know.

Now the moon is reigning as I seek the brightest star,
Clouds drift underneath like misty vapor from the tar,
Unwritten ancient histories and secrets left unknown,
Truly great events pass through the universe unshown.

Many miracles happened in the days of Godly times,
Windswept deserts held the key to all that was sublime,
Everyone will pass back into the great eternal mass,
Only God himself can see if what we've done will last.

"ABIGAIL"

When driving up a starry,
And winding country road,
As Indian summer's night,
Fell down in papery loads,
I looked ahead and saw,
A yellowish lamp-lit room,
Up on the second floor,
The fixture eerily loomed.

How cozily quaint the room,
Then suddenly appeared,
The brick two-story home,
I readily revered,
An historic, picture-esque,
And sturdy, old household,
A deep lamenting story,
Was waiting to be told.

In a rustic pub,
I sat down in a booth,
An old man made an entrance,
Looking quite aloof,
I introduced myself,
To the weather-beaten man,
To my surprise he cordially,
And tightly shook my hand.

I asked about the lamp-lit window,
On the shop filled street,
The fireplace began to glow,
With charcoaled, radiant heat,
The fury eyebrows of the man,
Suggested grave concern,
He told me the sad story,
And this is what I learned.

The lovely Skippack summers,
Had many shades of green,
Branching limbs of maple trees,
In rocky, mossy scenes,
The Perkiomen creek,
Wound lazily through the town,
A resonance of bliss,
A young heart always found.

Rowing down the creek,
Were Abigail and her fiancé,
Dragonflies swooped gracefully,
In rippling waterways,
Oaks reflected up,
From deeper sections of the creek,
Hopes sublimely floated by,
As raindrops fell down quick.

The night before the wedding,
She had the strangest dream,
She's swimming underwater,
In a tannish, caverned scene,
When coming to a boulder,
She moved it with great might,
A ghostly labyrinth,
Was lit by candlelight.

The mermaid felt unsure,
In this deep sea setting,
She swam into a tunnel,
Where lizard eyes were fretting,
She chased the fish-like creature,
To the center of the earth,
The molten lava core,
Was waiting for rebirth.

The underwater fairy,
Then caught the scaly creature,
As it turned it shockingly,
Revealed her Andrew's features,
A violent fire burst,
The great reptilian head,
An avalanche ensued,
The creature lay there dead.

She tried to pick him up,
From flaming, crumbling ground,
The fiery red volcano,
Would soon be skyward bound,
She then swam toward a cliff,
Where sunbeams flickered down,
Kicking up with force,
She emerged in her small town.

A splendid coach of walnut,
Now came to take the bride,
The crisp November air,
Made parties move inside,
The princess bride looked stunning,
On this magic day,
Church bells rang as leaves,
Were twirled in windy sways.

Up a webby loft,
A dove flapped fiercefully,
The organist pulled a chain,
The bird was finally free,
The silence then was deafening,
As all searched for the groom,
A hush went up the aisle,
With much foreboding gloom.

For on this day sweet Abigail,
Was left there at the altar,
And though she sensed the truth,
She still refused to falter,
Her father and some others,
Said they'd hunt him down,
But soon the grief was met,
And Abigail came around.

Alas, resilience is the strength,
Of youthful, sturdy souls,
Maple crowns with blue sky domes,
Can end exacting tolls,
As September sunlight,
Flutters through a tree,
Abigail rebounded,
Quite miraculously.

As the days passed by,
The story became old,
But one more scene of cruel desertion,
Waited to unfold,
Once again our Abigail,
Was left at the church steeple,
Confusion, shock and disbelief,
Were shown by all the people.

For oh how many times,
Can a tender heart be broken,
With a faithful soul,
Still hearing promises spoken,
The Perkiomen seasons,
Slowly passed along,
But Abigail no longer,
Heard the robin's song.

Like a flock of starlings,
Heading out of town,
Optimism's poignant moments,
Didn't stay around,
Looking at the lamp-lit window,
For the girl they'd known,
This is where the greatest sorrows,
Waited to be shown.

The thing that most amazed me,
About the bedroom light,
It only shone on windy,
And lonely Skippack nights,
Although my friend assured me,
To not have any fear,
The house had been locked up,
And vacant thirty years.

"MIRACLES"

Every single thing I see,
Appears a wondrous miracle to me,
A rainy rippling waterway,
A stormy leaf-blown autumn day.

The reaping of the harvest grain,
The fecund ways of blossomy days,
A succulent fare the soil brings,
With gathered piles of a sumptuous spring.

Baskets filled to the brim with fruit,
A carnation crop of rainbowed hues,
Beautifully textured roundish goods,
Wait patiently by the straw and wood.

And in the distance a freight-train song,
An iron horse a good mile long,
The coal cars shake the tiny bridge,
The tracks run toward a mountain ridge.

Late at night you'll hear the horn,
Of the midnight train weary and worn,
The diesel rolls through fields and streets,
But snug in bed you'll sleep with ease.

The cicada's call is a wondrous sound,
With deep green branches reaching down,
At night the crickets sing their song,
Hot, lazy summer days are long.

A newly painted cinder track,
Three relay teams run down the back,
Two lovers cross the soccer field,
Their youthful passions soon will yield.

A cardinal, bluejay and two doves,
And then the vow of lifetime love,
A month-old baby wrapped in cotton,
These are the things never forgotten.

"FEAR NOT"

Oh the sorrows this heart has known,
Only saved by heroic joy,
Then what is a man with no travails at hand,
And playing the shadowy decoy.

The body is strong for only so long,
Timidity toward the soil is ungallant,
When there's no mountain for us to assail,
Mediocrity becomes all too salient.

Boldness in the face of adversity,
Is a journey often taken alone,
Obstacles collide on a crowded, bleak path,
And some things are never atoned.

A lack of response from a flaccid heart,
Won't raise us above the soft crowd,
Better to run when the rest walk slow,
And better to shout clamorously loud.

Though man is only important to man,
And life is an unbending line,
Born out of all this struggle and strife,
Will be us standing tall and sublime.

"NEED"

Dismal feelings can smother me,
When I think of the forlorn ways of life,
Every friendship will eventually end,
As the strident time-clock turns its bend.

Poignant thoughts of old, lost scenes,
No longer warm my cloud-filled heart,
Even the glowing, colored trees,
Can't put my restless mind at ease.

Grasping for something so abstract,
Sadly knowing I'll never go back,
Pursued by a chilling relentless tide,
Seeking a place in which to confide.

Compassionate shoulders dry my tears,
Going alone is the greatest fear,
Help me find my way today,
Promise me right here you'll stay.

"BOLD"

Be bold like a rolling river,
Overtaking her stalwart bank,
Be brave like the rundown soldier,
Who confronts his enemy's tank,
Beware of false temptation,
Untrue friendship and bogus love,
Look down to gain perspective,
Never fear to scan above.

Be bold like a seasoned shepherd,
Guiding his keep across foggy hills,
Be brave like the old man dying,
Who holds on with all his will,
Beware of foolish pride,
Senseless goals and weakening strife,
Look up when things get weighty,
Never fear one day of life.

Be bold like a weathered sailor,
Heading into a rainy gale,
Be brave like the poverty-struck woman,
Who prays that her kin prevail,
Beware of superficial Gods,
And worrisome thieves of precious time,
Look in your soul for solitude,
Never fear to be sublime.

"LITTLE WHITE BUTTERFLY"

Little white butterfly,
How do you flutter in the wind,
And still reach your destination,
Your care-free flight,
From yard to yard,
Is a wondrous and cheerful sensation.

Gallivanting down the tree lined street,
Flying through golden and dusty sunbeams,
You bring magic to the soft and blooming day,
With your fast and unpredictable ways.

Dancing branch to branch quite wistfully,
In the blowing grass blade forest,
Landing on a mountain of shrubbery,
You're an anxious spring-time tourist.
Your precise navigation through fences and gates,
Lead to new worlds of blossoms and flowers,
Meandering through paradise in a spirited way,
You find solace in a soft rainbow shower.

Camouflaging yourself in a snowy pear tree,
You surprise me with every new movement,
Dodging fast cars and tall telephone poles,
Your frivolity could stand some improvement.
Landing on top of a dandelion stem,
Or exploring the buds of some clover,
Your escapes are quite quick and spontaneous,
As I slyly but slowly walk over.

The two stenciled dots on your trace paper wings,
Can be seen as you visit a red azalea,
Then two of you perform a sweet, circular ballet,
As you greet the sunshine on a warm, glowing day.
Can you clear the reflective, blue sky maple,
Or the candy pink dogwood and tulip tree,
The joy of rebirth is the background stage,
And your performance is heavenly glee.

"OH YOUTHFUL JOY!"

Oh youthful joy with thou wrinkle free smile,
Enlighten my world and sit here a while,
Flying around like a brisk butterfly,
Watch your balloon fly up into the sky.

Living the moment is your carefree call,
Adventurous roamings and tales that are tall,
Inside an igloo you hide with a friend,
A snowman keeps guard though it's just make-pretend.

You find fascination in each nook and cranny,
A miniature tea party with your old Granny,
Grown-up cuisine you approach with a sneer,
Cookies and candy you welcome with cheers.

An Easter egg hunt or a Holy Communion,
The primary star of the family reunion,
Ready to love and to learn without thinking,
Dancing with glee while I ponder my blinking.

Picture books are what you cherish the most,
Jelly and jam on your Saturday toast,
Running and sledding and climbing a tree,
Hiking with Robin Hood's men merrily.

"ARABIA"

As slumberous moments released inner thoughts,
A stroll on a monumental boardwalk occurred,
An oceanic mountain of surf then appeared,
Beachcombers ran fast as the tidal wave neared.

How dramatic and loud the encroaching sea was,
Burying the sand and threatening the land,
The boards were still safe as the wind whistled by,
Around the coastline sailed an ominous sky.

I'm treading a salty and warm waterway,
Thousands of trailers parked cozily in wet sand,
The egg smell of seaweed brings seagulls to bay,
Grassy mounds dry as the breeze makes them sway.

Night has arrived on the festive promenade,
People are speaking but I don't hear the words,
The aroma of wood and fresh peanuts is good,
Coming to a turn like the one in North Wildwood.

Exploring the lonely and timbered walkway,
Amazed by the vast and reflective dark sea,
An iron expansion bridge makes an appearance,
Under it moon waves roll by with much clearance.

Approaching a stormy and paved loading dock,
A tired sandbar sits behind a huge ship,
My business soon takes me aboard the strange vessel,
A siren sounds off in the seaway I'm nestled.

Standing above a clay Middle East town,
It's late as I scope the Moroccan-like scene,
I then grab two handles and ride a steel wire,
Tomorrow Arabia, but tonight a warm fire.

"THE TREES, THE TREES"

The trees, the trees,
Sometimes they speak to me,
They tell me tall tales,
Of past love and intrigue
They show me the way,
To reach up for the sky,
And they shade me in summer,
When the long days get dry.

They hover on top of the big, old stone house,
The place where we work for a penny or two,
We sit at their feet and rest a bit,
The wind gently blows as the sky becomes blue,
Seldom do we see the old owner of the estate,
It's lonely and quiet at the mansion of late,
I take my round shovel and rake in hand,
And look in the window as the shadows expand.

Not long ago I loved so deeply and strong,
My feelings ran deep as the ravine is long,
How I cherished each moment and savored each meeting,
But you never found love in my adoring greeting,
My dream slowly unfolded as a brown leaf flutters,
The words you told me made my kind soul shutter,
I knew I'd never have you to hold and embrace,
Our lives would never intercept face to face.

As I stare up at the tulip trees,
With my gaze directed heavenly,
I realize just how small I am,
And how we age so suddenly,
Knowing love is not always having love,
But as long as I can rise above,
I'll have my dream, though now with tears I choke,
As I esteem the tall, bulky oak.

"THE ROAD"

I've traveled down that bitter road,
Of weighty thoughts that overload,
A fragile soul not worldly worn,
Where feelings are so deeply torn.

I've walked the windswept road of life,
With all its careworn cumbrous strife,
Not knowing where I headed for,
But still surviving one day more.

I've searched for that one special love,
A dark-haired angel from above,
Sweet thoughts of when our lips might meet,
I've traveled far on this sad street.

And now I've reached that mountain top,
Where buried yearnings never stop,
One face to smile away the pain,
Two eyes to make me love again.

"THE PHILOSOPHERS"

It was a strange thing indeed,
When I met my friend Toby,
You see Toby it seemed,
Had the same dreams as me.

'Twas an odd-looking mirror,
With great similarity,
It's an eerie kind of feeling,
Seeing things objectively.

But Toby had a system,
Not just a fairy-tale dream,
He shared his cosmic blueprint,
It made good sense to me.

We'd sit out under the stars,
And contemplate our lives,
Other dreamers joined in,
Listening closely by.

Toby's dad would join us,
A black and wise old man,
Toby himself had freckles,
And a lighter sandy tan.

The old guy really knew the world,
And told us many stories,
Our back-yard meeting would convene,
The old man in his glory.

Warmly understated,
With a Pall-Mall in his hand,
He taught us many timely truths,
In ways we'd understand.

Toby and I would sit on the hood,
Of the Fairmount he had bought,
Lampposts shined down like a play,
Each word weighty with thought.

Toby liked the things I said,
His thoughts were beyond me,
In layman's terms it all seemed right,
With a midnight summer breeze.

Late-night meetings in the tiny yard,
Ended after summer break,
Toby and his family moved far away,
I hope he did find what it takes.

"SNOW MOUNDS"

An uncanny feeling I have for this jazz tune,
Profoundly familiar in a sad, haunting way,
A dark winter's day I look onto my past,
My role model gone as the flurries rise fast.

Three long years since I spoke to the old man,
He always had both good and bad things to say,
Profuse olden times intermingle in my heart,
Way back in those days seemed an auspicious start.

A late night snowfall and a walk to Woolworth's lot,
The snow mounds were magic to my brothers and I,
The sleepy small town lay beneath a crystal sky,
We'd climb every hill as the night passed us by.

Prolonged evening calls haunted us for a while,
He was gone but he needed to know if we loved him,
Of course we did, he would always be our Dad,
We'd visit him at work and he seemed so glad.

A bereaved heart I have now that we are estranged,
Stubborn fortitude only goes its lonely way,
I look at old ice mounds black with hurt pride,
My destiny lost as the cold grows inside.

"AWAKEN"

Reawaken your heart my friend,
Some inspiration I can lend,
The ancient oak has wisdom too,
The noble stuff will see you through.

A jet flies high and sings its call,
A wondrous thing seeing it all,
The cool air from the creek relieves,
A winding trail will greet the breeze.

A pond now greets a Mallard pair,
The valley has great secrets there,
A rusty train rolls by the road,
The fresh-cut grass and sweetgum blow.

At night you'll hear the freight-train pass,
A soothing sound until the last,
The textures of the drifty trees,
Make time go by with tranquil ease.

Awaken to the moon at dawn,
With clover snowflakes on the lawn,
The bustling town has noisy wares,
This time you'll take more than your share.

"OLD MAN BILL"

Old Man Bill gave us all a big chill,
To look in his eyes took a lot of free will,
Haggard deep sockets with a scrawny, long beard,
Those old army boots were the thing we most feared.

He lived down in the old shack by the tracks,
The freight trains passed by the junky old back,
A pile of old tires and ladders and wood,
Some rusty old metal and an antique car hood.

The house didn't look very fine on good days,
A sad house it was in a neglectful way,
A jumbled one-floor stretch of partitioned rooms,
The overgrown garden was all doom and gloom.

See Bill was a drinker and stank of strong wine,
His sense of direction was a little behind,
Soon all us kids took it on our sweet selves,
To escort him home when he got on the shelf.

Those hot summer nights we had fun hittin' the skids,
We played in his yard smashing old trashcan lids,
He sometimes would talk to us real kind and wise,
The thing he most feared was the cruel, old sunrise.

Old Man Bill had an old dog named Phil,
A grungy old mut who preferred stayin' still,
We counted on Phil to take charge when we left,
The canine himself seemed concerned and bereft.

Well things stayed the same for a while I suppose,
Bill stayed hung over for God only knows,
Then one sunny day a strange thing occurred,
Inside the house a young girlfriend now stirred.

Quite pretty and young at least next to old Bill,
His drinkin' and bummin' well she'd had her fill,
The place got cleaned up and the grass finally cut,
She treated us nice when we came to our hut.

How can I explain Bill's great transformation,
His beard and his hair were trimmed back each location,
You see old Bill wasn't as old as we thought,
He was just in his forties and a little distraught.

Next thing you know Bill was workin' again,
His clothes got cleaned up but he stayed our dear friend,
An amazing thing indeed what a little love can do,
It's a new day for him and a new one for you.

"ROBOTS"

I wasn't sure if it was a robot,
Who drove by me the other day,
With a phone attached to his head,
And a dreamy-eyed, vacant face.

A lot of these robots are roaming,
Having intense conversations with themselves,
They seem to have some vague yearning,
Though apparently unaware of much else.

I don't really want to be a part of,
Their innermost thoughts and concerns,
They seem to enjoy jumbo vehicles,
In which precious fossil fuels burn.

Many of them live in great boxes,
Where rooms go unfurnished for years,
Rage ushers in the new morning,
And feelings are felt without tears.

A computerized man is a strange thing,
As a pure northern wind passes by,
The country hills beckon me over,
And I let it all go with a sigh.

"A THOUGHT"

The northern red-winged blackbirds,
Had a wonderful camaraderie,
Painted crimson birthmarks,
Fluttering closely knit for seed.

A colorful traveling flock,
With many chicks beside the old,
Belonging to their own kind,
As in nature it is told.

A sudden, synchronized dodging,
The starlings made when landing,
A fluttery image to last all time,
As speeding clouds passed by.

A serious gathering of fluorescent wings,
With their changing purplish hues,
Pecking into the moistened soil,
And finding plentiful food.

Everyone must tend to their own,
This is what must be,
The kinder ways will take front stage,
When caring for the weak.

Battle looms in Jerusalem,
Across the wavy seas,
Easter day I always pray,
God's children will be free.

"SPARROW SONG HEART"

Enchanted exuberance the sparrows display,
As they bob to and fro on this November day,
They switch back and forth from their designated shoots,
They sing and they whistle and let out their hoots.

The fluffy little rascals take turns at the seed,
During split-second shifts they continue to feed,
Soon a northerly wind makes a vibrating sound,
And they scatter like bats to bare trees with a frown.

I remember in Niagara how the sparrows ran free,
Hopping through gardens with an unrefrained glee,
Pitter-patter they danced on the walkways like clowns,
As the tall Norway Maples grew heavenly bound.

Two moths fly by and I feel quite surprised,
They are happily together for the winter I surmise,
Two fluttering spirits in a sweet eternal flight,
A butterfly joins them on the last buds of life.

The frost paints a glassy white sheet everywhere,
The furry squirrels bury their acorns with care,
A copper beech shivers in the crisp autumn glaze,
My passion rebounds when I see nature's ways.

I feel very happy on these Merion Square streets,
Stone mansions of old with great sycamore leaves,
A coat of fresh snow soon will lay on the grass,
My sparrow song heart helps the icy months pass.

"A RUSTIC TALE"

(The Tale of Bible Boy)

A rustic tale I have to tell,
Though it may not be for all,
A tale about a Bible boy,
Who stood 'round six feet tall,
Bible boy was an ambitious builder,
Of great things big and small,
Always with him was his Bible,
In case of a fiery fall.

His father was a hardened drunk,
And walked a ruined road,
Two Scandinavian brothers soon,
Would have the same fate told,
One younger brother appeared real slow,
The other was bulby-head sad,
Two pretty sisters completed the clan,
And they both appeared almost glad.

In the midst of a hot, hazy day,
On top of the old avenue,
Bible boy and a young negro girlfriend,
Were having a brief interlude,
Strolling along the quaint privet hedges,
And reading a scripture or two,
They seemed in a world unto itself,
Quite tranquil and very subdued.

Bible boy had a pleasant-type face,
With a thin and dungereed frame,
A face that asked many questions,
With his eyes a little enraged,
Blondishly slender and tall like a worker,
His forehead was beady with thought,
Swinging his hammer and reading the word,
Is what the boy earnestly sought.

Like the Lord's son, Bible boy was a builder,
And beautiful things he bestowed,
Small wooden boxes for trinkets and treasures,
And chests made of walnut and oak,
But the greatest achievement of Bible boy's work,
Was a fortress behind the long yard,
Hammering nails while measuring and cutting,
And not with one piece to discard.

Back on those lazy, bright summer days,
I'd cut through the crab-apple yards,
Bible boy was very proud of his fort,
On which he had worked very hard,
Bible boy's mother would gleam as she stood,
Beside her young preachin' son,
Everyone there'd be praisin' him for,
The good work of God he had done.

A Lincoln log passage gave us our entrance,
To cozy and shelved tiny rooms,
Inside the hidden and snug wooden fort,
Was almost as dark as a tomb,
Seated inside I'd watch creeping sunlight,
Fight its way into the door,
Dusty sunbeams would sneak through the cracks,
As I sat on the plywood floor.

Wirey fences and sinewy trees,
Kept guard at this magical place,
Privet growth hung right over the roof,
As Harrison sang about grace,
A secret cut-through between the two yards,
Led into an old parking lot,
Those peaceful times inside the log cabin,
Were good and I forgot them not.

What the coming months and years would bring,
I still didn't really know,
Cartoons reigned as childhood flowed,
And back then things went slow,
But the wilder ones had secret plans,
Toward Bible boy's new fort,
Often they'd sneak in with booze,
And hold their devilish court.

The freckled ones came home from church,
One restless and sad day,
Bible boy and his family,
Had driven far away,
What then ensued was terrible,
Too horrific to explain,
The fort was badly damaged,
In great fits of boyish pain.

A robin sang an early song,
As dewy lawns lay down,
In the distance a hammer beat,
As delivery men came 'round,
Bible boy now spent his time,
Rebuilding with fresh wood,
He forbore through the turmoil,
In a meek and tireless sainthood.

Bible boy and his negro girlfriend,
Continued their afternoon walks,
Labor day snuck up some way,
And came with boards and chalk,
Bible boy would end his life,
At the end of a climbing rope,
But in his death I only see,
Great wisdom and great hope.

"LOVER"

When you ceased to be my lover,
How the sky fell down,
The weight of many cold gray days,
I carried them around,
Spontaneous naked bedside meetings,
Ended all too soon,
The rapture of your skin on mine,
No more my interlude.

You said I took for granted,
All the warmth that you bestowed,
Your soft embracing breasts,
My cheek again would never know,
The passion dance of arms and torsos,
Reaching down below,
Now made time become detached,
As sorrows crept by slow.

How I glided like a bird,
Enthralled by every phrase,
Many untold fates took hold,
Behind love's murky haze,
Only half without the whole,
Of love's most tender ways,
The hand I held so tightly,
Now was gone without a trace.

One brief kiss could make the day,
Go lightly sailing by,
Dreaming each new moment,
I'd again be by your side,
Adroitly in control of every thought,
Within my heart,
You somehow were the moon and sun,
Without even a start.

Now the day is a study,
On the empty ways of life,
Though resilience in my soul,
May soon regain its stride,
Unrequited love a prison flower,
Wilted and dry,
Once the seed has grown,
There's no escape from the inside.

"UNKNOWN"

Newly found feelings of gleeful sweet bliss,
Sometimes bring sadness and great emptiness,
The tenderest excitement can die in one night,
But love's many whims often take their own flight.

Those brief magic moments that highlighted my days,
Brought great happiness in sunny sky ways,
Your every smile filled my entire galaxy,
My heart was brought back to a time long unseen.

Promising glimpses I saw in each expression,
Your long wondrous hair gave a lasting impression,
But the cruel essence of your disdain for my eyes,
Was suddenly unhidden by a fearful disguise.

My desire was bold though it took a great toll,
Resolution succumbed when I sacrificed my soul,
The spring-time of joy lasted one moment more,
When the kindness of love turned a painstaking chore.

Rapturous tranquility was only inside of me,
The road that was chosen embittered me miserably,
My life came undone as a chill ate my bones,
The fate of you now is a thought turned unknown.

"WAITING FOR SPRING"

Sometimes I look back,
On special moments and old times,
Eternity beckons me,
As inner feelings turn sublime,
The wonder of the summer,
Soon will soothe and pacify,
The cold rain chills the soil,
But the noon sun rises high.

Then I stare across,
The sunny hay-brown field,
A group of robins gather by,
The church as winter yields,
A giant flock of starlings,
Soon takes the neighborhood,
They bob around like fighters,
From oak and gingko wood.

The lovely springtime flowers,
Paint a pastel on the grass,
My soul will be enchanted,
As the temperatures rise fast,
Walking by a gentle pine,
That sings a soft tone song,
A row of shady ferns,
Will grow leafy and long.

I'm hoping soon that everything,
Turns green yet once again,
It's been a tiresome season,
And my spirits on the mend,
A squirrel with a white belly,
Digs acorns from the fall,
He climbs a leafless Pin Oak,
With bulky branches tall.

Every frosty morning,
I look out and dream of spring,
The dogwoods and magnolias,
Will be coronated kings,
The silver spotted starlings,
And robins came today,
Cherry blossoms soon,
Will greet me on my way.

"NIAGARA"

From far away Niagara,
I can hold you in my hands,
Two funneling mountains of mist,
Creating a canyon oh so grand.

I'll never forget the sound,
Of fierce rapids that first night,
And the steepened water's edge,
With its rainbowed candlelight.

An Atlantean symbol of might,
Where Neptune held his court,
Releasing his trident downstream,
To the whirlpool and its sort.

Triton's trumpet rings,
Through frosty blue ice flows,
A misty rising heaven,
Above the undertow.

Niagara you're so far,
But still you own my heart,
Someday I will return,
To where all dreams can start.

"YOUR SONG"

Yes, I love You,
More than the sun
loves his clear blue sky,
More than the moon
loves his ocean tide.

Yes, I love You,
More than the seagull
loves his seaside perch,
More than Columbus
loved his immortal search.

If not, I'll sail,
into the lonely sea,
If not, I'll go,
If I mold a new soul,
We'll see.

Yes, I love You,
More than the bird
loves his morning song,
More than the general
loves his brave and strong.

Yes, I love You,
More than the deer
loves his wooded home,
More than Michelangelo
loved his marble dome.

If not, I'll sail,
Into the lonely sea,
If not, I'll go,
If I mold a new soul,
We'll see.

"STARRY NIGHT"

Starry night,
You look over the sea,
Tell me why, the dream is done.

Sorry day,
You were waiting there for me,
Now I know that she is gone.

How I wish,
She would come back and see,
All the things we left undone.

Now I know,
That our love just can't be,
Now today, I must move on.

Starry night,
You look over the sea,
Tell me now, is she alright.

Sorry day,
Won't you please comfort me,
Will I see her once again.

How I wish,
She would come home to me,
She was gone much too soon.

Now I know,
That I'll never be free,
She was made, just for me.

"AUTUMN SCENES"

Golden views of pastel hues,
Orange domes with skies of blue,
Gorgeous yellow tints of green,
Maples in a coral scene.

Intricate strokes for Monet's sea,
Fluffy rainbowed grand relief,
A phosphorescent golden fleece,
Etched-on branches underneath.

Amber snowflakes floating down,
Dreamy drifting homeward bound,
Crispy glowing resolution,
Burgundy oaks shedding fruition.

"THE LIGHTNING BUGS"

When sitting by the garden at twilight in July,
The magical arrival came of a thousand fireflies,
So luminously lovely were their yellow flickering lights,
A glorious transition for a long day's restful night.

A little flying seahorse quickly came over to play,
As the eastern sky began to change to gray,
Reminding me of a lighthouse stranded out at sea,
The tiny fairy gladly shared his fiery beam.

Conjuring up pictures of a deep sea submarine,
The contrast with the foliage was eerily pristine,
Abundant silent secrets he candidly displayed,
Then several of them formed a Halloween parade.

Natural and free bright pulsating flights,
Some chose the maple trees to camouflage their lights,
Soon I made a wish then took my lonely leave,
The starry depth of nature I readily perceived.

"THE CROW"

The crow didn't know or at least didn't show,
That behind him was a blue sky full moon,
High up above on his sinewy dead tree,
The blowing green fields were a pondering sea.

Flapping down in a phantasmagoric swoop,
Breaking away from his small eerie troop,
He stepped to the birdbath quite effortlessly,
He took a quick drink then a noise made him flee.

A true loner with an inquisitive soul,
A medieval cape on an old grassy knoll,
The rook soon returned to his straggly dead limb,
The moon glowed without as the crow stood within.

"CHURCH BELLS"

Back when I was young,
And underneath a gentle sun,
I always enjoyed the sounds,
Of church bells in the distance,
And though I didn't know,
Just how quickly life would go,
The timeless tower's chiming,
Was filled with sweet bright notes.

Only a freight train rolling by,
Could make a better sound,
Thunder, lightning or a great snowstorm,
They also came around,
A windy high school marching band,
Parades into the zone,
Rustling leaves blow spirally,
On the chilliest day yet known.

Beside the locomotive's song,
The church bells soothed me well,
Especially in a boy's world,
With medieval tales to tell,
Fluffy sparrows in the trees,
Couldn't match the metallic tones,
Or all those sparkly Christmas tunes,
I savored as my own.

On cloudy, lonely days the chimes,
Could somehow make things right,
On late October evenings,
They would summon in the night,
When snow filled up the rooftops,
They would ring to cancel school,
A joyous celebration,
Throwing iceballs damp and cool.

The fire siren rings and shakes,
The tiny town's foundation,
Invading Martian ships,
Or a great nuclear penetration,
Screaming fire trucks then squeeze,
Through narrow, hedge-filled streets,
We watch the ladder steerman make,
Another Herculean feat.

The bell for school would ring,
Across the morning dew,
We'd fly on concrete ramps,
As buses came in slews,
Obediently marching into rooms,
Of chalky, wooden hues,
We'd stare out windows dreamily,
With saddened eyes of blue.

The final day of school,
Was a heaven on the earth,
A time of liberation,
And a boyhood's sweet rebirth,
The three o'clock would sound,
And we'd trample steps with glee,
Papers flew on pavement,
As the buses helped us flee.

A flock of starlings lands,
On the old magnolia tree,
Their squeaking tones a deepened song,
Of tumultuous harmonies,
Mother's supper-bell then rings,
And down the limbs we climb,
Those dreamy boyhood days,
Were genuine and sublime.

Santa's bells could always win,
A place in my young heart,
And on a tinseled Christmas Eve,
The magic soon would start,
Looking out at snow-filled pines,
And hanging icicles,
Wondering just how life could be,
A snowy miracle.

Hanging yard chimes gently play,
On a Spring-time Easter day,
Mom and Dad are dressed,
In a sleek and elegant way,
Church bells send a song across,
The sleepy red-brick town,
Daffodils rise up to see,
The peace and love they found.

"EVERYTHING"

Oh to be young and alive and well,
With a future so bright and a dream to sell,
Conquering the world and knocking them dead,
Memorable moments are easily led.

I've felt those magic feelings before,
On gentle nights as I stood by the door,
In my first rowhome I felt assured,
Looking down from the tall second floor.

I'll never forget those special times,
When the silver maple had reason and rhyme,
A voice inside assured me somehow,
Worries aside I lived for the now.

Watching my daughter grow smart and sweet,
Breathing it in from the coldness to heat,
Being poor didn't stop me one bit,
The mysteries of life in my mind still fit.

Those were good days in my twenties and beyond,
You're only young once staring into the pond,
We'd walk the stone bridge to the foresty side,
Enchanted with life and no reason to hide.

"QUESTIONS"

Oh fleeting time,
Drifting by with a sigh,
The days come and go,
And we still don't know why.

Every deep moment,
Will soon dissipate,
Does everything get old,
Is this really my fate.

Does anyone know me,
Can they see in my soul,
Can it be that close,
Without any toll.

The sun shines down,
And makes the world gay,
But the sense and meaning,
Are so hidden away.

That dark-haired beauty,
Her smile is my sun,
Someday I'll show her,
How love has begun.

God must know,
How I still feel him near,
Perhaps he will show me,
Then all will be clear.

"OLD LOCUST TREE"

The old locust tree, cracked and thorny,
Each fissured ridge has a different story,
Of seasons gone and long forgotten,
Creviced limbs with a trunk half rotten.

But stand you will a four-score more,
Your eyes have seen a countless lore,
Prickly stickers and elongated seed,
Down below frozen papery leaves.

I stare in awe of your dismembered frame,
The pronounced bark is why I came,
The stone farmhouse you stand beside,
An old comrade with whom you confide.

I feel amazed looking up at you,
You speak when northern winds subdue,
Holding firm in a relentless storm,
A statuesque wisdom always the norm.

I truly say, I love you old tree,
Please be strong then eventually,
April's spring will come again,
A tale I'll tell around the bend.

"THE MALLARD DUCKS"

The Mallard ducks immersed their moist, hungry bills,
As an overreached sycamore oversaw and stood still,
With rippling gray waters and clouds overcast,
The entertainment of the feast inspired me fast.

Many times I had strolled down the tall treed lane,
The fluttering leaves fell when an autumn breeze came,
Glancing over the old, rotted blockade fence,
The forty-odd ducks' supper became more intense.

The beautifully feathered and royal green males,
As their golden bronze lovers watched on to no avail,
Dipped their heads in the creek quite resiliently,
Their fervor for living did astonish me.

As northern wind blew through high sprawling branches,
I shuddered and wept at my dwindling, last chances,
The passing years had become one long continuum,
As the hopes of my youth were now nearly done.

What singular, sad journeys we all must take,
But the elegance of these birds I could now not forsake,
For I knew that God's landscape must have infinite grace,
And I knew I'd be well in this deep, wondrous place.

"THE OLD MAN"

The old man lived alone,
He played the fiddle well,
He did his best to stay away,
From ever getting too involved,
This is what I know.

Way back in the small town,
We'd go and hunt him down,
He'd tell us things about old times,
When he was young and he could fight,
This is what I know.

Why oh why sweet baby,
Why oh why sweet baby, go!

We'd trim his hedge each month,
And sit out drinkin' cokes,
He'd play a tune, we'd sit and watch,
He'd pay us each a buck or two,
This is how it goes.

The years passed by real fast,
The old man stayed alone,
The little house behind the hedge,
Still standing there but no one cares,
This is how it goes.

Why oh why sweet baby,
Why oh why sweet baby, go!

"THE CANADIAN GEESE"

Late in December as I treaded the frost,
A spellbound faint echo trickled down from above,
A deep haunting song in the dark, twilight sky,
I surveyed and searched obscure heavens by and by.

At last I alighted upon a momentous boomerang,
Of loud, honking dragons ascending to the stars,
The Canadian geese formed a clangorous chorus,
They soared easily through the cone-filled pine forest.

Now the great flock traveled out of my view,
With deep voices falling on the tree tops and roofs,
I wondered where these noble birds could be flying,
To a far-away land where the wind is still sighing.

"TIP THE SCALE"

Precious moments often come,
When they're least expected,
A clear-eyed resolution is,
An ephemeral moment of truth.

The translucent rained-on shrubbery,
Reflects and shimmers like crystal,
The cicada's song is a trembling vibrato,
Put on this earth to soothe.

The Canadian geese stagger me,
With a sudden, flapping orbit,
Artistic bodies majestically rise,
In pure, uproarious flight.

My soul is swept with the infinity,
Of tree-tops endless pondering,
Their shivery fluctuations,
A forest of deep insight.

The mutability of every breath,
Confounds me with a sigh,
I watch the wind gently caress,
Two phosphorescent trees.

A papery grasshopper runs away,
Displaying painted wings,
Then a flittery white butterfly,
Tips the scale for earthly peace.

"CLOUD FORMATIONS"

A farmhouse of stone stood back on the field,
The ancient woodpile was still and alone,
Ahead lay a snowcapped Mount Everest sky,
The moon and the stars formed a grandiose dome.

A Himalayan mass of lavender clouds,
Rose over the horizon in Vesuvian style,
Dandelions woke to see the strange scene,
The mythic dark ridge stood high up a mile.

A harvest wind blew the tall, unkept weeds,
Two rabbits concluded their early night feast,
The volcanic setting was epic in scope,
With galaxies flying above jagged peaks.

A dark gaseous passage across the great earth,
I cherished this biblical Pompeian place,
Glaciers floated by the Alaskan canal,
Soon I lost track of all time and space.

My mind was enthralled by wonderful sights,
An old cherry tree spoke quietly to me,
The transient Van Gogh night vista was glowing,
As worries from daytime became vaporous glee.

"A GHOSTLY TALE"

A velvet red rose trembled,
Under a papery autumn haze,
The breeze blew rustling leaves,
Into mysterious old tideways,
The sun sat like a pumpkin,
In a sky that seemed brand new,
I wistfully stared at sinewy trees,
Of haunting reddish hues.

October is the time when furry squirrels,
Rake up with brooms,
Their work intensifies,
Under thick skies of frosty gloom,
A few leftover thistle-downs,
Enjoy tumultuous rides,
A ghostly little white butterfly,
Rides a northern wind in stride.

Jack-O-Lanterns go on hunts,
For long-nosed warty witches,
A cold and rainy night is the prime time,
For horror twitches,
Twilight's when the fun begins,
With witch-strewn fuzzy moons,
Excitement brews as ghostly spirits,
Sing their trembling tunes.

The cottage sat behind the green,
And virtually was unseen,
The dark Victorian house was where,
Old vampires would convene,
An eerie ship-wreck wind blew,
Across the desolate beach,
Any sign of summery cheer,
Was officially out of reach.

Vines had overtaken the yard,
In one fell swoop of death,
Ivy crept up cracking walls,
And into the chimney's breath,
A creaky iron gate led into,
A jungled, weedy path,
Only brave souls enter here,
Was the agreed-on epitaph.

Drifty darkish clouds were sailing,
Around a werewolf moon,
It made the old house ethereal,
While apprehending doom,
With just one day to Halloween,
We craved a phantom thrill,
We hid behind two spindly trees,
And knelt there very still.

We shuddered at an evergreen,
And watched for demon eyes,
An old crow seemed to call to us,
Behind his dark disguise,
He landed on the porch and then,
He grew into a man,
He scoped the graveyard vines,
And into a mist he then expanded.

Tracy and I shivered,
As the blood rushed to our heads,
Too afraid to run we now,
Were trapped within our dread,
Suddenly a wolf ran by,
Beneath fragmented moonlight,
He stood on two clawed feet,
And disappeared from earthly sight.

The shocking final visitor,
Was a pompous alley cat,
When we looked real close,
We saw his cape and stylish cap,
He stood up like a man,
And turned into an old-world vampire,
Looking around suspiciously,
To the kitchen he retired.

After a haunting eternity,
We snuck up toward the house,
Strange bombastic dialogue,
Sent tremors through a mouse,
Creeping up toward webby brush,
We peeked within the window,
A spider dropped down pensively,
As candles spookily glowed.

The wolf, the crow and alley cat,
Though shaped like humans below,
Retained their original heads,
And on cigars they vigorously smoked,
A good card game is why they came,
As a knocking sea-wind blew,
They played each hand strategically,
As shadows eerily moved.

I have to say the unarming way,
In which these comrades played,
Reminded me of olden days,
When my aunts and uncles stayed,
Playing cards is always fun,
On a haunted, shivery night,
Staring at this laughing bunch,
Could almost calm my fright.

But something stirred, I don't know what,
And chaos then ensued,
The crow, the wolf and alley cat,
Were gone in a mist of blue,
A lamppost glowed most gloomily,
On this cold night in Cape May,
Walking down the cobblestones,
We headed on our way.

"THE HERMIT'S CALL"

I've had enough blind supplication,
Endeavoring hard to make them smile,
Sacrificing my tenuous dignity,
Craving approval all the while.

Are you surprised I changed my ways,
I walk a new-found road today,
Slowly fading from the scene,
Better to leave than aimlessly stay.

Friends just hamper my natural growth,
Everyone wants to call it their own,
I've heard too much of the theories and chatter,
My special place will be all alone.

Now my new life slowly begins,
Shedding my skin like a big, old snake,
Sharing my moods and speaking the truth,
I'll stay alive and be awake.

The hermit's call isn't bad after all,
It's a peaceful journey to a private place,
Don't be upset when the clown retires,
Underneath you'll find his trace.

"A FEW THINGS"

A gentle war it is between the sun and wind,
A January day fends off a restless spring,
Soft Pacific air helps fight the bitter flow,
Rolling fields display pastel etchings of snow.

In spring I'll be intrigued by a distant, sunny field,
Beyond the line of trees and viney, bristled shield,
The meadow will imbue a dewy fresh sunlight,
Robins will return with stormy rain-filled nights.

The early morning breeze of a gentle summer's day,
Will bring a sparrow's song in an old familiar way,
A leafy dome-shaped maple will stand up on a hill,
The cicada's call returns while camouflaging still.

In fall the maples turn into a vast rainbow,
Look and then you'll see each color that you know,
Papery leaves are strewn on frosty lawns of green,
These are just a few things I have lately seen.

"SANDS OF TIME"

When my soul awakens,
Do I then accept my end,
And all the souls around me,
Will they live yet once again.

Can these petty grievances,
Be laid to rest at last,
Or will the flaws within my mind,
Enslave me to the past.

I have to say I've lost my way,
Though not every moment's sad,
I still believe in coming joys,
And look on ones I had.

Somewhere in between the shadows,
Lives a joyous soul,
Shady summer afternoons,
Before life took its toll.

I don't know how I got to here,
In this vacuum standing still,
Watching all of life go by,
Without exerting my will.

Bring me back to olden days,
When life had reason and rhyme,
Poignant moments stood alone,
In the wondrous sands of time.

"THISTLEDOWNS"

Chasing around thistledowns is a grand thing indeed,
Running to and fro in the tall summer weeds,
But catching one is no easy matter my friend,
An empty set of hands you'll have in the end.

Lighter than air, not forthcoming with a breeze,
These infinite escapes are made with graceful ease,
People just don't have the quickness and the skill,
To grab fleeting time and make it stand still.

As a boy I'd run in the middle of the street,
Chasing a white furry down I would never meet,
It seemed just when victory was at my fingertips,
A current would then lift it onto a sky-bound trip.

Watching them is truly the pleasure of it all,
Enraptured with the wind and delicate and small,
Floating in a curious way and not with one concern,
Sneaking through a fence or making a sudden turn.

Perhaps we weren't meant to physically connect,
Maybe you disintegrate before we intercept,
See my kind is clumsy and burdened with thought,
Eternity for you is so easily sought.

"SIGNS"

Vaporescent icy mist,
Was haunting on the drive,
Twirling clouds ephemerally,
Like lost ghosts intertwined,
Sunlight gives these spirits life,
Until the coldness ends,
Rising into drifting forms,
When warmer air descends.

Evanescent sights intrigue me,
In their changing states,
Signs of supernatural beings,
Touch me as of late,
Where do all the people go,
When they're dead and gone,
The knowing ones who sat with us,
As the night grew long.

A leaning frozen forsythia,
Is a mass of icicles,
Connected phosphorescent spaces,
Gleam like shiny walls,
Could spirits really live within,
This shivery-layered flow,
Escaping in the tiny drops,
Onto the melting snow.

Might they beam their shadows,
On the dormant winter trees,
Glowing through the ridgey bark,
Within a thawing breeze,
Or rippling through a melting pond,
Onto a Mallard bill,
These enchanted happenings,
I'm watching closely still.

"MY TROLLEY RIDE"

My magic lifetime trolley ride,
Imbued with a mystical, churning tide,
Will take you down a wooded slope,
A valley view of spirited hope.

The tracks descend through a leafy ravine,
A field beyond the trees pristine,
The windowed sky with emerald domes,
Where fluffy clouds and wings can roam.

By a bouldered cliff the trolley speeds,
With hidden caves and prickly weeds,
On top two boys watch closely by,
The approaching train will make them sigh.

A nickel is laid on top the track,
And now the kids come running back,
A surreal half-dollar they retrieve,
Climbing back on bikes they leave.

Joy-filled years float happily by,
And still we love the trolley line,
Hazy days swimming in the old creek,
Climbing maples mossy and thick.

The trolley glides through viney yards,
With wooden sheds and abandoned cars,
And then through fields with power lines,
My crystalline view at times sublime.

The trolley took me to college when I grew,
High on a cliff the railcar flew,
Great thinkers and writers I came to know,
Enchanting days would come and go.

Cascading leaves on the raindrops of time,
And now I behold a little girl of mine,
The station sits cozily behind old stores,
The trolley glides by a field of back doors.

These wonderful days I do miss them so,
The spring and the robin, the autumn and snow,
Quaint narrow streets with sycamore trees,
Old weeping cherries and a lavender breeze.